Awaken Your Inner Spirit

Discovering the Path to True Enlightenment and Inner Peace

Tristan Richards

Table of Contents

Chapter 1

The Foundations of Inner Spirit

Defining Inner Spirit

Inner spirit is an elusive concept that has captivated humanity for centuries. It represents the core of our being, the essence that transcends physical existence and connects us to a higher plane of consciousness. Understanding and defining inner spirit is crucial for anyone embarking on a journey towards enlightenment and inner peace. At its heart, the inner spirit is the purest expression of our true self, untainted by external influences or societal expectations.

The concept of inner spirit can be traced back to ancient civilizations. In various cultures, it has been referred to as the soul, the essence, or the divine spark within each individual. The ancient Egyptians believed in the "ka," a spiritual double that accompanied a person throughout their life and into the afterlife. In Hindu philosophy, the "atman" is considered the innermost essence, identical with Brahman, the ultimate reality. Similarly, in Christianity, the soul is viewed as an immortal entity that embodies a person's true nature and connection to God.

Despite the diverse terminologies and interpretations, a common thread runs through these beliefs: the inner spirit is a timeless, transcendent force that defines who we are beyond our physical form. It is the source of our deepest wisdom, intuition, and moral compass. While our bodies and minds are subject to change and decay, the inner spirit remains constant and eternal.

Modern science has also begun to explore the concept of inner spirit, albeit through different lenses. Neuroscientists and psychologists investigate the nature of consciousness, seeking to understand the relationship between the brain and the subjective experience of self. Research in positive psychology highlights the importance of spiritual well-being for overall mental health, suggesting that a strong sense of inner spirit can lead to greater resilience, purpose, and life satisfaction.

Mindfulness plays a significant role in nurturing and connecting with our inner spirit. By cultivating present-moment awareness, we can peel back the layers of distraction and illusion that obscure our true self. Mindfulness practices, such as meditation and breath awareness, help quiet the mind and create space for the inner spirit to emerge. This process requires patience and dedication, but the rewards are profound: a deeper sense of clarity, authenticity, and inner peace.

In today's fast-paced, materialistic world, many people feel disconnected from their inner spirit. The constant bombardment of information, societal pressures, and external validation can drown out the subtle voice of our true self. Reconnecting with the inner spirit often involves unlearning conditioned behaviors and beliefs that no longer serve us. It requires a willingness to explore the depths of our being, confront our fears, and embrace our vulnerabilities.

Spiritual growth practices can aid in this journey of reconnection. These practices vary widely, reflecting the diverse paths to inner spirit across different cultures and traditions. Common practices include meditation, prayer, journaling, and spending time in nature. Each of these activities offers a unique way to tune into the inner spirit and cultivate a deeper sense of self-awareness.

Meditation, for instance, is a powerful tool for accessing the inner spirit. By sitting in stillness and focusing the mind, we can transcend the ego and connect with the deeper layers of our consciousness. There are many forms of meditation, from guided visualizations to mantra repetition, each offering a different pathway to the inner spirit. Regular meditation practice can help quiet the mental chatter, reduce stress, and foster a sense of inner calm.

Prayer is another practice that can strengthen our connection to the inner spirit. While often associated with religious traditions, prayer can also be a personal, non-denominational practice. It involves communicating with a higher power or the universe, expressing gratitude, seeking guidance, and affirming our intentions. Through prayer, we can cultivate a sense of surrender and trust, allowing the inner spirit to guide us on our path.

Journaling is a reflective practice that can help uncover the voice of the inner spirit. By writing down our thoughts, feelings, and experiences, we can gain insights into our true self and identify patterns that hinder our spiritual growth. Journaling can be a form of self-dialogue, providing a safe space to explore our innermost desires, fears, and aspirations. It encourages honesty and vulnerability, essential qualities for spiritual awakening.

Nature has long been revered as a source of spiritual inspiration and healing. Spending time in natural settings can help us reconnect with the inner spirit by grounding us in the present moment and reminding us of our interconnectedness with all life. Whether it's a walk in the forest, a hike in the mountains, or simply sitting by a river, nature provides a sanctuary for introspection and renewal.

The beauty and tranquility of the natural world can awaken a sense of awe and reverence, opening the door to deeper spiritual experiences.

The journey to define and connect with the inner spirit is deeply personal and unique to each individual. There is no one-size-fits-all approach, and what works for one person may not resonate with another. It's important to explore different practices and find what resonates with your own inner truth. Trusting your intuition and being open to experimentation can lead to profound discoveries and transformations.

As we delve deeper into the nature of the inner spirit, we may encounter resistance and challenges. The process of awakening often involves confronting our shadow self—the aspects of our personality that we have repressed or denied. This can be uncomfortable and even painful, but it is a necessary step towards wholeness. Embracing our shadow allows us to integrate all parts of ourselves, leading to greater self-acceptance and compassion.

Community and support are also vital in the journey of defining and nurturing the inner spirit. Sharing our experiences with others, whether through spiritual groups, workshops, or trusted friendships, can provide encouragement and insights. A supportive community can help us stay motivated, offer different perspectives, and remind us that we are not alone on this path.

Ultimately, defining the inner spirit is an ongoing process of self-discovery and growth. It requires a commitment to living authentically, aligning our actions with our deepest values, and continuously seeking to understand and express our true self. As we cultivate a stronger connection with our inner spirit, we can navigate life's challenges with greater ease, find meaning and purpose in our experiences, and contribute to the well-being of others.

Historical Perspectives on Spirituality

Spirituality, a concept deeply embedded in the human experience, has evolved significantly over millennia. From ancient civilizations to modern times, the ways in which people understand and seek spiritual fulfillment have been shaped by cultural, religious, and philosophical contexts. Examining historical perspectives on spirituality not only illuminates the diverse expressions of human spirituality but also provides insight into the universal quest for meaning, connection, and transcendence.

Ancient Egypt, one of the earliest cradles of civilization, offers a profound example of spirituality interwoven with daily life and governance. The Egyptians believed in a pantheon of gods and goddesses, each embodying different aspects of the natural world and human experience. Spirituality was not confined to temples or rituals; it permeated every aspect of society. The concept of Ma'at, representing truth, balance, and cosmic order, was central to Egyptian spirituality. Pharaohs, seen as divine intermediaries, were responsible for maintaining Ma'at through their rule. The afterlife played a crucial role in Egyptian spirituality, with elaborate burial practices and tombs designed to ensure a safe passage and eternal life. The Book of the Dead, a collection of spells and prayers, guided the deceased through the afterlife, highlighting the Egyptians' intricate beliefs about the soul's journey beyond death.

In ancient India, spirituality found expression through the Vedic traditions, which later evolved into Hinduism. The Vedas, composed around 1500 BCE, are a collection of hymns, rituals, and philosophical teachings that form the foundation of Hindu spirituality. Central to these teachings is the belief in the atman, or the inner self, which is eternal and identical with Brahman, the ultimate reality. The pursuit of understanding this unity is the essence of spiritual practice in Hinduism. Over time, various paths to spiritual realization emerged, including Bhakti (devotion), Jnana (knowledge), and Karma (action). The Upanishads, composed between 800 and 400 BCE, delve deeper into the nature of reality and the self, presenting profound philosophical insights that continue to influence spiritual seekers today.

Buddhism, founded in the 5th century BCE by Siddhartha Gautama, the Buddha, brought a transformative perspective on spirituality. The Buddha's teachings, known as the Dharma, emphasize the Four Noble Truths and the Eightfold Path as the way to overcome suffering and achieve enlightenment, or Nirvana. Unlike the theistic traditions of the time, Buddhism focuses on personal experience and inner transformation rather than worship of deities. Meditation, mindfulness, and ethical conduct are core practices in Buddhism, aiming to cultivate wisdom, compassion, and inner peace. As Buddhism spread across Asia, it adapted to various cultural contexts, giving rise to diverse schools such as Theravada, Mahayana, and Vajrayana, each with unique spiritual practices and interpretations.

In ancient Greece, spirituality was closely tied to philosophy and the quest for knowledge. The pre-Socratic philosophers pondered the nature of existence, the cosmos, and the divine. Socrates,

Plato, and Aristotle further developed these inquiries, exploring the relationship between the human soul and the universe. Plato's theory of the Forms posited a realm of perfect, eternal ideals, of which the material world is a mere shadow. The soul's journey, according to Plato, involves recollecting these ideals and striving for a higher state of being. Aristotle, on the other hand, emphasized the importance of virtue and practical wisdom in achieving eudaimonia, or flourishing. The Hellenistic period saw the rise of schools such as Stoicism and Epicureanism, which offered different paths to spiritual well-being. Stoicism, with its focus on rationality, self-control, and acceptance of fate, has experienced a resurgence in modern times as a practical philosophy for navigating life's challenges.

The monotheistic traditions of Judaism, Christianity, and Islam each brought unique perspectives on spirituality, centered around the belief in one God. In Judaism, spirituality is deeply rooted in the covenantal relationship between God and the people of Israel. The Torah, containing the law and teachings, guides Jews in their spiritual practice, emphasizing justice, compassion, and the sanctity of life. The concept of Tikkun Olam, or repairing the world, highlights the Jewish commitment to social justice and ethical living as expressions of spirituality.

Christianity, emerging in the 1st century CE, centers on the life and teachings of Jesus Christ. His message of love, forgiveness, and redemption resonated deeply, leading to the establishment of a spiritual community that emphasized faith, hope, and charity. The early Christian church developed various spiritual practices, including prayer, sacraments, and monasticism, as means of cultivating a closer relationship with God and living out the teachings of Christ. The mystics of the medieval period, such as St. John of the Cross and St. Teresa of Avila, explored the depths of spiritual experience through contemplative prayer and union with the divine.

Islam, founded in the 7th century CE by the Prophet Muhammad, offers a comprehensive framework for spiritual and ethical living. The Qur'an, considered the literal word of God, provides guidance on all aspects of life, from personal conduct to social justice. The Five Pillars of Islam—faith, prayer, fasting, charity, and pilgrimage—constitute the core practices that shape a Muslim's spiritual journey. Sufism, the mystical branch of Islam, seeks direct experience of the divine through love, devotion, and inner purification. Sufi poets like Rumi and Hafiz have expressed profound spiritual insights through their poetry, emphasizing the unity of all creation and the transformative power of divine love.

The Enlightenment period in Europe marked a significant shift in spiritual perspectives, as reason and scientific inquiry began to challenge traditional religious beliefs. However, this era also saw the development of new spiritual movements that sought to reconcile reason with spirituality. Transcendentalism, led by figures like Ralph Waldo Emerson and Henry David Thoreau, emphasized the inherent goodness of people and nature, advocating for self-reliance, individual conscience, and a direct connection to the divine. The Romantic movement, with poets such as William Wordsworth and Samuel Taylor Coleridge, celebrated the spiritual beauty of nature and the power of the imagination.

In the 20th century, spirituality continued to evolve, influenced by global interconnectedness and the exchange of ideas across cultures. The rise of the New Age movement brought together elements from various spiritual traditions, emphasizing personal growth, holistic health, and the exploration of consciousness. Eastern practices such as yoga, meditation, and mindfulness gained widespread popularity in the West, offering new pathways to spiritual fulfillment. Psychologist Carl Jung's exploration of the collective unconscious and the spiritual dimension of the psyche provided a bridge between psychology and spirituality, encouraging individuals to seek wholeness through inner exploration.

The Science Behind Inner Peace

Inner peace, often described as a state of mental and emotional tranquility, is a profound and universally sought-after experience. It is the quieting of the mind, the calming of emotional turbulence, and the attainment of a balanced state of being. While the concept of inner peace is frequently discussed within spiritual and philosophical contexts, science offers a robust framework to understand the mechanisms behind it. By examining the interplay between brain function, psychological practices, and lifestyle choices, one can uncover practical strategies to cultivate and sustain inner peace.

The human brain, a complex organ responsible for thoughts, emotions, and behaviors, plays a crucial role in the experience of inner peace. Neuroscience reveals that different areas of the brain are involved in regulating stress, emotions, and relaxation. The amygdala, for instance, is central to the processing of fear and anxiety. When faced with a perceived threat, the amygdala activates the body's fight-or-flight response, releasing stress hormones like cortisol and adrenaline. While this response is vital for survival, chronic activation due to everyday stress can lead to heightened anxiety and disrupt inner peace.

Conversely, the prefrontal cortex, located at the front of the brain, is associated with higher-order functions such as decision-making, impulse control, and emotional regulation. Research shows that engaging the prefrontal cortex through mindfulness practices can reduce the activity of the amygdala, thereby mitigating stress responses. Mindfulness, the practice of paying non-judgmental attention to the present moment, has been extensively studied for its calming effects on the brain. MRI scans of individuals who regularly practice mindfulness meditation reveal increased gray matter density in the prefrontal cortex and other regions linked to emotional regulation and self-awareness.

Another significant aspect of the brain's role in inner peace is the default mode network (DMN), a network of brain regions that becomes active when the mind is at rest and not focused on the external environment. The DMN is involved in self-referential thinking, daydreaming, and rumination. While it plays a role in creativity and problem-solving, excessive activity in the DMN can lead to overthinking and negative self-talk, which are detrimental to inner peace. Practices such as meditation and deep breathing exercises have been shown to reduce DMN activity, promoting a more serene mental state.

Beyond the brain's structure and function, the concept of neuroplasticity underscores the potential for cultivating inner peace. Neuroplasticity refers to the brain's ability to reorganize itself by forming new neural connections throughout life. This adaptability means that with consistent practice, individuals can rewire their brains to favor calmness and resilience over stress and anxiety. Techniques such as cognitive-behavioral therapy (CBT) leverage neuroplasticity by helping individuals identify and change negative thought patterns, thus fostering a more peaceful mindset.

Psychological practices also play a pivotal role in achieving inner peace. One such practice is gratitude, the act of recognizing and appreciating the positive aspects of life. Studies have shown that gratitude can significantly enhance well-being and reduce stress. When individuals focus on what they are grateful for, they activate brain regions associated with reward and positive emotions, such as the ventromedial prefrontal cortex. Keeping a gratitude journal, where one regularly writes down things they are thankful for, can help shift focus away from negative thoughts and cultivate a more peaceful state of mind.

Another effective psychological practice is self-compassion, which involves treating oneself with kindness and understanding in times of failure or difficulty. Research by psychologist Kristin Neff indicates that self-compassion is linked to lower levels of anxiety and depression and higher levels of life satisfaction. Self-compassion practices often include self-kindness (being gentle with oneself), common humanity (recognizing that suffering is a shared human experience), and mindfulness (observing thoughts and feelings without judgment). By fostering a compassionate inner dialogue, individuals can reduce self-criticism and promote inner peace.

Lifestyle choices, encompassing diet, exercise, and sleep, also significantly impact inner peace. Nutrition plays a crucial role in brain health and emotional regulation. Diets rich in omega-3 fatty acids, antioxidants, and vitamins have been shown to support cognitive function and reduce inflammation, which is linked to mood disorders. Foods such as fatty fish, nuts, fruits, and vegetables can nourish the brain and contribute to a balanced mental state. Conversely, excessive consumption of sugar and processed foods can lead to mood swings and anxiety, undermining inner peace.

Physical exercise, another vital component of a peaceful lifestyle, has well-documented benefits for mental health. Exercise increases the production of endorphins, the body's natural mood elevators, and promotes the release of neurotransmitters such as serotonin and dopamine, which are associated with happiness and well-being. Regular physical activity also reduces levels of cortisol, the stress hormone, and can improve sleep quality. Activities like yoga and tai chi, which combine physical movement with mindfulness, are particularly effective in promoting inner peace.

Sleep, often overlooked, is essential for emotional regulation and cognitive function. Chronic sleep deprivation can lead to irritability, impaired judgment, and heightened stress levels. Ensuring adequate and quality sleep supports brain function and emotional resilience. Establishing a consistent sleep routine, creating a restful sleep environment, and avoiding stimulants like caffeine before bedtime can enhance sleep quality and contribute to a more peaceful mind.

The role of social connections in fostering inner peace cannot be overstated. Human beings are inherently social creatures, and meaningful relationships are fundamental to emotional well-being. Social support provides a buffer against stress and promotes a sense of belonging and security. Engaging in positive social interactions releases oxytocin, a hormone that reduces stress and enhances feelings of trust and bonding. Cultivating healthy relationships, seeking support during challenging times, and participating in community activities can significantly enhance inner peace.

Moreover, spiritual or religious practices often provide a framework for achieving inner peace. For many, spirituality offers a sense of purpose, connection to something greater than oneself, and a source of comfort during difficult times. Practices such as prayer, meditation, and participation in religious rituals can foster a sense of inner calm and resilience. Studies have shown that individuals who engage in regular spiritual or religious practices report higher levels of life satisfaction and lower levels of anxiety and depression.

In addition to these practices, the environment in which one lives and works can influence inner peace. Creating a peaceful physical environment, free from clutter and conducive to relaxation, can have a positive impact on mental well-being. Natural light, plants, and calming colors can enhance the ambiance of a space and promote a sense of calm. Spending time in nature, whether through walking in a park or hiking in the mountains, has been shown to reduce stress and improve mood. Nature exposure can lower cortisol levels and increase feelings of awe and connectedness, contributing to inner peace.

The Role of Mindfulness

Mindfulness, a practice rooted in ancient contemplative traditions, has gained widespread recognition in contemporary society for its profound impact on mental well-being. It involves paying deliberate, non-judgmental attention to the present moment, fostering a heightened state of awareness. This chapter delves into the role of mindfulness in enhancing mental health, reducing stress, and improving overall quality of life. By understanding its principles and integrating practical techniques, individuals can harness the power of mindfulness to navigate the complexities of modern living with greater ease and clarity.

The origins of mindfulness can be traced back to Buddhist meditation practices, where it was considered a path to enlightenment. However, in the past few decades, mindfulness has been secularized and integrated into Western psychology and medicine. One of the pioneers in this field is Jon Kabat-Zinn, who developed the Mindfulness-Based Stress Reduction (MBSR) program in the late 1970s. MBSR combines mindfulness meditation and yoga to help individuals manage stress, pain, and illness. Kabat-Zinn's work has been instrumental in bringing mindfulness into mainstream healthcare and demonstrating its benefits through rigorous scientific research.

At its core, mindfulness is about cultivating an awareness that is both focused and expansive. It requires observing thoughts, feelings, and bodily sensations without getting caught up in them or reacting impulsively. This practice can be likened to standing on the bank of a river, watching the water flow by without being swept away by the current. By maintaining this observer stance, individuals can gain insights into their habitual patterns of thinking and behaving, which often contribute to stress and unhappiness.

One of the primary benefits of mindfulness is its ability to reduce stress. Chronic stress is pervasive in modern society, contributing to a range of physical and mental health problems, including hypertension, anxiety, depression, and weakened immune function. Mindfulness interrupts the stress response by promoting relaxation and enhancing emotional regulation. Studies have shown that mindfulness practices can lower levels of cortisol, the body's primary stress hormone, and increase activity in brain regions associated with positive emotions and self-control.

Mindfulness also plays a significant role in improving mental health. It has been effectively incorporated into various therapeutic approaches, such as Mindfulness-Based Cognitive Therapy (MBCT) and Acceptance and Commitment Therapy (ACT).

MBCT, for example, combines mindfulness practices with cognitive-behavioral techniques to prevent relapse in individuals with recurrent depression. By encouraging individuals to become more aware of their thoughts and feelings, MBCT helps them recognize early signs of depression and take proactive steps to manage it.

In addition to reducing stress and improving mental health, mindfulness enhances cognitive functioning. Regular mindfulness practice has been shown to improve attention, memory, and executive function. This is attributed to the practice's ability to strengthen the prefrontal cortex, the brain region responsible for higher-order cognitive processes. Enhanced cognitive function not only boosts productivity and performance but also contributes to a greater sense of well-being.

Another significant aspect of mindfulness is its impact on emotional intelligence. Emotional intelligence involves the ability to recognize, understand, and manage one's own emotions, as well as the emotions of others. Mindfulness fosters emotional intelligence by promoting self-awareness and empathy. Through mindful observation, individuals can become more attuned to their emotional states and learn to respond to them in a balanced and constructive manner. This, in turn, improves interpersonal relationships and communication.

In practical terms, integrating mindfulness into daily life does not require significant time investment or drastic lifestyle changes. Simple practices, such as mindful breathing, body scan meditation, and mindful eating, can be incorporated into everyday routines. Mindful breathing involves focusing attention on the breath, observing its natural rhythm without trying to control it. This practice can be done anywhere and anytime, providing a quick and effective way to center oneself and reduce stress.

The body scan meditation is another powerful mindfulness practice. It involves systematically directing attention to different parts of the body, observing sensations without judgment. This practice not only promotes relaxation but also enhances body awareness, helping individuals identify areas of tension and discomfort. Over time, the body scan meditation can improve the mind-body connection and promote a greater sense of physical and emotional well-being.

Mindful eating, on the other hand, encourages individuals to bring full awareness to the experience of eating. This involves paying attention to the colors, textures, and flavors of food, as well as the sensations of hunger and fullness. By eating mindfully, individuals can develop a healthier relationship with food, reduce overeating, and enhance their enjoyment of meals. This practice also highlights the interconnectedness of mindfulness with other aspects of health and well-being.

For those new to mindfulness, starting with short, guided meditations can be helpful. Numerous apps and online resources offer guided sessions that range from a few minutes to longer periods. These sessions provide structure and support, making it easier to establish a regular practice. As individuals become more comfortable with mindfulness, they can gradually increase the duration and explore different techniques.

Mindfulness can also be integrated into daily activities beyond formal meditation. Everyday tasks, such as walking, washing dishes, or driving, can be opportunities for mindfulness practice. By bringing full attention to the present moment and engaging all the senses, individuals can transform mundane activities into moments of mindful awareness. This approach not only enhances the quality of these experiences but also reinforces the habit of mindfulness.

In the workplace, mindfulness has been shown to improve job satisfaction, reduce burnout, and enhance performance. Many organizations now offer mindfulness training programs to their employees, recognizing the benefits of a mindful workforce.

These programs often include practices such as mindful breaks, mindful listening, and stress management techniques. By fostering a culture of mindfulness, organizations can create a more supportive and productive work environment.

Mindfulness also has a positive impact on physical health. Beyond its effects on stress and mental well-being, mindfulness has been linked to improved cardiovascular health, enhanced immune function, and better pain management. For individuals with chronic conditions, mindfulness can provide a valuable tool for managing symptoms and improving quality of life. The holistic benefits of mindfulness underscore its potential as a complementary approach to conventional medical treatments.

The role of mindfulness in fostering resilience is another area of growing interest. Resilience, the ability to adapt and thrive in the face of adversity, is crucial for navigating life's challenges. Mindfulness enhances resilience by promoting emotional regulation, reducing reactivity, and fostering a sense of inner calm. Through mindful practices, individuals can develop a greater capacity to cope with stress, recover from setbacks, and maintain a positive outlook.

Modern Practices for Spiritual Growth

Modern spiritual growth practices are as diverse as the individuals who seek them. These practices integrate ancient wisdom with contemporary approaches, making spirituality accessible and relevant in today's fast-paced world. Spiritual growth is not confined to any one religion or belief system; it is a personal journey towards greater self-awareness, inner peace, and connection with the universe. This chapter delves into various modern practices that foster spiritual growth, offering practical guidance for beginners and experienced seekers alike.

One of the most significant modern practices for spiritual growth is meditation. While meditation has ancient roots in traditions such as Buddhism and Hinduism, its contemporary forms are varied and adaptable to different lifestyles. There are numerous types of meditation, including mindfulness, transcendental, loving-kindness, and guided meditations. Each type offers unique benefits, but all share the common goal of quieting the mind and connecting with a deeper sense of self. For beginners, starting with a simple mindfulness meditation can be particularly effective. This involves sitting quietly and focusing on the breath, gently bringing the mind back whenever it wanders.

Over time, this practice can lead to a greater sense of calm, clarity, and spiritual awareness.

Journaling is another powerful tool for spiritual growth. Keeping a journal allows individuals to reflect on their thoughts, feelings, and experiences, providing a space for introspection and self-discovery. Writing about one's spiritual journey can help clarify beliefs, set intentions, and track progress. Many people find that journaling in the morning sets a positive tone for the day ahead, while others prefer to write in the evening to reflect on the day's events. Prompts such as "What am I grateful for today?" or "What challenges did I face, and how did I grow from them?" can guide journaling sessions and deepen the practice.

Yoga, with its blend of physical postures, breath control, and meditation, is a holistic practice that supports spiritual growth. Beyond its physical benefits, yoga encourages mindfulness, self-discipline, and a connection to the present moment. Each pose, or asana, can become a moving meditation, fostering a deeper connection between the body, mind, and spirit. Many practitioners find that regular yoga practice enhances their overall sense of well-being and spiritual awareness. Whether attending a class or practicing at home, incorporating yoga into one's routine can be a transformative experience.

Another modern practice that fosters spiritual growth is the use of affirmations. Affirmations are positive statements that individuals repeat to themselves to reinforce desired beliefs or outcomes. They can be particularly powerful when used consistently, helping to reprogram the subconscious mind and cultivate a more positive and empowered mindset. Examples of affirmations for spiritual growth include "I am connected to the divine source of the universe," "I trust the journey of my life," and "I am open to spiritual growth and transformation." Repeating these affirmations daily, either silently or aloud, can help align one's thoughts and actions with their spiritual aspirations.

Nature immersion, or spending time in natural environments, is another effective practice for spiritual growth. Nature has a unique way of grounding us, reminding us of the interconnectedness of all life. Whether it's a walk in the park, hiking in the mountains, or simply sitting by a river, being in nature can provide a profound sense of peace and clarity. Many people find that nature immersion helps them feel more connected to the earth and the greater universe, fostering a sense of awe and reverence for life. This practice can also be combined with other activities, such as meditation or journaling, to enhance its benefits.

For those seeking community and connection, joining a spiritual group or attending spiritual retreats can be incredibly enriching. Many people find that sharing their spiritual journey with others provides support, inspiration, and a sense of belonging. Spiritual groups can take many forms, from meditation circles and yoga classes to book clubs and discussion groups focused on spiritual topics. Retreats, whether for a weekend or longer, offer immersive experiences that can deepen one's practice and provide valuable insights. These gatherings often include a mix of activities such as meditation, yoga, workshops, and group discussions, creating a supportive environment for spiritual exploration and growth.

Another practice gaining popularity in modern spirituality is the use of crystals and gemstones. Many cultures throughout history have believed in the healing and spiritual properties of crystals. Each type of crystal is thought to offer different benefits, such as promoting love, protection, or clarity. Incorporating crystals into one's spiritual practice can be as simple as carrying a stone in one's pocket, meditating with it, or placing it in a space where its energy is needed. While the scientific basis for crystal healing is debated, many people find that working with crystals enhances their spiritual practice and provides a tangible focus for their intentions.

Breathwork, the practice of consciously controlling the breath, is another powerful tool for spiritual growth. Different breathwork techniques, such as pranayama, holotropic, and transformational breathing, offer various benefits, from stress reduction and emotional release to altered states of consciousness and spiritual insights. Breathwork sessions can be guided by a practitioner or practiced independently once the techniques are learned. The act of focusing on the breath can help quiet the mind, release stored emotions, and connect with a deeper sense of self and the universe.

Modern spiritual growth also involves the cultivation of gratitude. Practicing gratitude shifts focus from what is lacking to what is abundant in one's life, fostering a more positive and content mindset. This can be done through simple daily practices, such as keeping a gratitude journal, where one writes down things they are thankful for each day, or mentally acknowledging moments of gratitude throughout the day. Over time, cultivating gratitude can transform one's perspective, making it easier to find joy and meaning in everyday experiences.

Sound healing, which uses sound frequencies to promote healing and spiritual well-being, is another contemporary practice. This can include listening to music, chanting, using singing bowls, or participating in sound baths. Sound has the ability to influence our brainwaves, promoting relaxation and altered states of consciousness. Many people find that sound healing helps them to release emotional blockages, reduce stress, and enhance their spiritual awareness. Incorporating sound healing into one's routine can provide a soothing and transformative experience.

Finally, modern spiritual growth often involves the integration of ancient wisdom with contemporary science. Practices such as mindfulness-based stress reduction (MBSR), developed by Jon Kabat-Zinn, combine meditation with scientific understanding of the mind and body. This integration makes spiritual practices more accessible to a wider audience and provides a framework for understanding their benefits in a modern context. By bridging the gap between ancient and modern, these practices offer a holistic approach to spiritual growth that is both timeless and relevant.

Chapter 2
Preparing for the Journey

Setting Intentions

Setting intentions is a powerful practice that helps to align one's actions with their deepest desires and goals. Unlike mere goal-setting, which often focuses on specific outcomes, setting intentions is about the underlying purpose and the energy you bring to your actions. This practice can transform how you approach life, providing a sense of direction and clarity that enhances both personal and spiritual growth.

At the heart of setting intentions is the idea of mindfulness. Being present and aware of your thoughts, feelings, and actions allows you to consciously choose your path. Start by finding a quiet space where you can reflect without distractions. Take a few deep breaths to center yourself. This moment of stillness is crucial, as it allows you to connect with your inner self and listen to what truly matters to you. Think about your core values and what you genuinely want to bring into your life. Is it peace, love, abundance, or perhaps personal growth? These reflections will guide you in forming your intentions.

Writing down your intentions can make them more concrete and actionable. Use a journal or a dedicated notebook for this purpose. Begin by stating your intention in a positive and present tense, as if it is already happening. For example, instead of saying, "I want to be less stressed," you might write, "I am calm and centered." This positive framing helps to shift your mindset and align your subconscious with your conscious desires. Be clear and specific, but also allow flexibility for how your intentions might manifest.

Visualization is a powerful technique to reinforce your intentions. Spend a few moments each day visualizing your intentions as if they are already a reality. Close your eyes and imagine the sights, sounds, and feelings associated with your intention. If your intention is to cultivate more joy, picture yourself in a joyful state, surrounded by people and activities that make you happy. This mental rehearsal can create a strong emotional connection to your intention, making it easier to stay focused and motivated.

Affirmations are another tool that can support your intentions. Create short, positive statements that reflect your intentions and repeat them daily. For example, if your intention is to foster self-love, you might use affirmations like, "I am worthy of love and respect," or "I love and accept myself unconditionally." Repeating these affirmations can help to rewire your thinking patterns and keep your intentions at the forefront of your mind.

It's essential to revisit and reflect on your intentions regularly. Life is dynamic, and your needs and desires may change over time. Set aside time each week or month to review your intentions and assess your progress. Reflect on what has been working well and what might need adjustment. This practice of regular reflection ensures that your intentions remain relevant and aligned with your current circumstances.

Incorporating rituals into your intention-setting practice can add a deeper sense of meaning and commitment. Rituals don't have to be elaborate; they can be simple actions that you perform with intention and mindfulness. Lighting a candle, for instance, can symbolize bringing light and clarity to your intentions. Some people find that incorporating elements of nature, such as stones, flowers, or water, helps to ground their intentions and connect them to the natural world. Choose rituals that resonate with you and make them a regular part of your intention-setting practice.

Sharing your intentions with a trusted friend or a supportive community can amplify their power. Speaking your intentions out loud to someone else can make them feel more real and create a sense of accountability. It also opens the door for support and encouragement from others who are invested in your growth. If you're comfortable, consider joining a group or community where members share and support each other's intentions. This collective energy can be incredibly motivating and inspiring.

Mindfulness practices, such as meditation and yoga, naturally complement the process of setting intentions. These practices help you to cultivate a state of presence and awareness, making it easier to connect with your true desires. During meditation, you can focus on your intention, allowing it to permeate your thoughts and feelings. Yoga, with its emphasis on breath and movement, can help to embody your intentions physically. As you move through your practice, you can dedicate each pose or breath to your intention, creating a holistic connection between mind, body, and spirit.

It's important to approach intention-setting with a sense of openness and non-attachment. While it's essential to be clear and specific about what you want, it's equally important to remain open to how your intentions might manifest. Sometimes, the universe has plans that are even better than what we can envision. Trust the process and be willing to adapt as needed. This balance of clarity and flexibility allows your intentions to unfold naturally and in alignment with the greater good.

Self-compassion is a crucial aspect of setting and pursuing intentions. It's easy to become critical of yourself if things don't go as planned or if progress seems slow. Remember that setting intentions is a journey, not a destination. Be kind to yourself and acknowledge every step you take, no matter how small. Celebrate your successes and learn from any setbacks without judgment. This attitude of self-compassion will keep you motivated and resilient on your path.

Gratitude also plays a significant role in the practice of setting intentions. By cultivating an attitude of gratitude, you can attract more positive experiences and align your energy with abundance. Take time each day to acknowledge and appreciate the progress you have made towards your intentions. This practice of gratitude can shift your focus from what's lacking to what's already present in your life, creating a positive feedback loop that supports your intentions.

Finally, remember that setting intentions is an ongoing practice. It's not something you do once and forget about. Make it a regular part of your life, integrating it into your daily or weekly routines. The more consistently you practice setting and nurturing your intentions, the more you will see their impact on your life. It's a dynamic process that evolves with you, offering endless opportunities for growth and transformation.

Creating a Sacred Space

Creating a sacred space is an essential practice for cultivating inner peace, reflection, and spiritual growth. This space serves as a sanctuary where you can retreat from the chaos of daily life and connect with your innermost self. It is a place dedicated to tranquility and intention, designed to support your practices, whether they be meditation, yoga, journaling, or simply moments of stillness.

The first step in creating a sacred space is to choose a location that feels right for you. It doesn't have to be an entire room; a corner of a room, a spot in your garden, or even a small nook can suffice. The key is that it should be a place where you feel comfortable and where you can be undisturbed. Consider the natural light, the noise levels, and the overall atmosphere of the location. A space with good natural light can be uplifting, while a quieter area can enhance your ability to focus and relax.

Once you have chosen your location, the next step is to clear the space. Remove any clutter or items that do not contribute to a sense of peace and relaxation. Clutter can be distracting and can carry stagnant energy, which can interfere with the calmness you seek to create. Clearing your space is not just about physical tidiness; it's also about creating an environment that feels energetically clean. You might choose to smudge the area with sage or use essential oils to purify the space. This ritual can help to set the tone and intention for your sacred space.

Personalization is a significant aspect of creating a sacred space. Incorporate elements that resonate with you and support your practices. This could include items such as candles, crystals, plants, or meaningful objects that inspire you. Each item should hold significance and contribute to the ambiance you wish to cultivate. For instance, candles can bring a sense of warmth and illumination, while plants can introduce a touch of nature and growth. Crystals are often used for their energetic properties, and you might choose ones that align with your intentions, such as amethyst for clarity or rose quartz for love.

Consider the use of color in your sacred space. Colors have powerful psychological effects and can influence your mood and energy. Soft, muted tones like blues, greens, and earth tones can create a calming environment, while vibrant colors like reds and oranges can evoke energy and passion. Choose colors that make you feel the way you want to feel in your sacred space. Fabric elements like cushions, throws, or tapestries can also add texture and comfort, making your space more inviting and cozy.

Sound is another important element to consider. Whether it's the gentle hum of a fan, the soothing sounds of nature, or the calming tones of a sound bowl, incorporating sound can enhance the sensory experience of your sacred space. You might choose to have a playlist of meditative music, nature sounds, or even a small fountain for the tranquil sound of running water. These auditory elements can help to drown out external noise and bring you into a state of relaxation and focus.

Scent can also play a powerful role in creating a sacred space. Aromatherapy uses scents to influence mood and well-being. Essential oils, incense, or scented candles can infuse your space with fragrances that promote calm, focus, or whatever state you wish to cultivate. Lavender, for example, is known for its relaxing properties, while citrus scents like lemon or orange can be uplifting and energizing. Choose scents that resonate with you and enhance the atmosphere of your space.

Lighting is crucial in setting the mood for your sacred space. Natural light is ideal, but if that's not possible, consider using soft, warm lighting from lamps or candles. Avoid harsh, fluorescent lighting, as it can be jarring and counterproductive to creating a serene environment. Dimmer switches or adjustable lamps can give you control over the intensity of the light, allowing you to create the perfect ambiance for different activities.

Once your space is set up, it's important to establish a routine for using it. Consistency can help to reinforce the sacredness of the space and make it a powerful tool for your personal growth. Set aside regular times to retreat to your sacred space, whether it's for meditation, journaling, or simply sitting in quiet reflection. This routine can become a cherished part of your day, providing a sense of grounding and stability.

Mindfulness can be a key practice in your sacred space. Engage in activities that bring you into the present moment and connect you with your inner self. This could include meditation, breathwork, or mindful movement like yoga or tai chi. The goal is to use your sacred space as a place to cultivate awareness and inner peace. Over time, this practice can extend beyond your sacred space and influence how you interact with the world around you.

In addition to mindfulness, your sacred space can be a place for creative expression. Activities like journaling, drawing, or painting can be deeply therapeutic and can help you to process emotions and thoughts. Allow yourself the freedom to explore and create without judgment. Your sacred space is a safe haven where you can express yourself authentically and explore your inner landscape.

Another way to enhance your sacred space is by incorporating elements of nature. Plants, flowers, stones, and even small water features can bring the calming and rejuvenating energy of nature into your space. Nature has a grounding effect and can help to balance your energy. If possible, consider having a window with a view of the outdoors or placing your sacred space in a garden or outdoor area.

Finally, it's important to maintain your sacred space. Just as you would clean and care for other parts of your home, your sacred space deserves regular attention. This could include physical cleaning, like dusting and organizing, as well as energetic cleansing, like smudging or using sound to clear stagnant energy. By maintaining your sacred space, you keep it vibrant and conducive to your practices.

Tools for Spiritual Practice

Finding the right tools for your spiritual practice can significantly enhance your journey toward inner peace, self-discovery, and personal growth. These tools serve as aids to deepen your practice, helping to center your mind, open your heart, and connect with your spirit. They can be physical objects, techniques, or even rituals that resonate with you and support your spiritual endeavors.

Meditation cushions, or zafus, are among the most commonly used tools in spiritual practice. These cushions provide support and comfort during meditation, allowing you to maintain proper posture and stay seated for longer periods without discomfort. A zafu helps to elevate the hips, reduce strain on the back, and promote a stable sitting position. Different shapes and sizes are available, and choosing one that fits your body can make a significant difference in your meditation experience. Pairing a zafu with a zabuton, a larger cushion placed underneath, can further enhance comfort by cushioning the knees and ankles.

Incorporating a mala, a string of 108 beads traditionally used in Hinduism and Buddhism, into your practice can help you stay focused during meditation or prayer. Malas are used to count recitations of mantras or prayers, allowing you to concentrate more deeply and establish a rhythm. Each bead represents a single repetition, and the tactile sensation of moving from one bead to the next can be grounding and calming. Malas are made from various materials, including wood, seeds, gemstones, and crystals, each carrying its own unique energy and symbolism. Selecting a mala that resonates with your intentions can add a meaningful dimension to your practice.

Crystals and gemstones are revered for their energetic properties and can be powerful tools for spiritual practice. Each type of crystal is believed to possess distinct vibrations and qualities that can influence your energy and environment. For example, amethyst is often associated with clarity and spiritual insight, while rose quartz is linked to love and compassion. You can incorporate crystals into your practice by holding them during meditation, placing them on your altar, or carrying them with you throughout the day. Cleansing your crystals regularly, either by placing them in sunlight, moonlight, or using sound, ensures they maintain their energetic purity.

Sound can be a transformative element in spiritual practice, and there are various tools designed to harness its power. Singing bowls, often made of metal or crystal, produce resonant tones when struck or circled with a mallet. These tones can induce deep relaxation, facilitate meditation, and clear negative energy from a space. Tuning forks, gongs, and chimes are other sound tools that can create healing vibrations. Chanting mantras or prayers aloud is another way to use sound to elevate your spiritual practice, as the vocalization and repetition can help to align your mind, body, and spirit.

Essential oils and incense are aromatic tools that can enhance your spiritual practice by influencing your mood and energy. Essential oils are concentrated plant extracts that can be diffused, inhaled, or applied to the skin (with proper dilution). Each oil has unique properties; for instance, lavender is known for its calming effects, while frankincense is often used for spiritual grounding. Incense, made from aromatic plant materials, can be burned to purify the air, set the mood, or signify the beginning of a practice. Scents like sandalwood, sage, and palo santo are commonly used for their spiritually uplifting and cleansing qualities.

Journaling is a powerful tool for self-reflection and spiritual growth. Keeping a dedicated journal for your spiritual practice allows you to record insights, experiences, and progress over time. Writing can help to clarify your thoughts, process emotions, and set intentions. You might choose to journal after meditation, during a moon phase, or whenever you feel the need to reflect. Prompts can guide your writing, such as questions about your current state, aspirations, or areas of gratitude. Revisiting past entries can provide valuable perspective on your journey and highlight patterns and growth.

Altars serve as focal points for spiritual practice, providing a dedicated space to honor your intentions and connect with the divine. An altar can be as simple or elaborate as you like, often including items such as candles, statues, crystals, flowers, and photographs. The act of creating and tending to an altar is itself a form of devotion, helping to center your attention and create a sacred atmosphere. Changing the items on your altar to reflect the seasons, lunar phases, or personal milestones can keep your practice dynamic and aligned with the natural cycles.

Tarot and oracle cards are tools for divination and introspection, offering insights and guidance on your spiritual path. Each card in a tarot deck carries specific symbolism and meaning, and drawing cards can help to illuminate hidden aspects of yourself or situations. Oracle cards, while similar, tend to have more varied themes and can be used in a more intuitive and flexible manner. Regularly working with these cards can help to develop your intuition and provide a deeper understanding of your inner world. Keeping a journal of your readings can help track patterns and insights over time.

Using breathwork techniques, such as pranayama, can significantly enhance your spiritual practice by connecting you more deeply with your body and energy. Different breathing exercises can calm the mind, energize the body, or facilitate a meditative state. For example, alternate nostril breathing (Nadi Shodhana) balances the hemispheres of the brain and calms the nervous system, while Bhastrika (bellows breath) energizes and clears the mind. Incorporating breathwork into your daily routine can bring immediate benefits and support your overall spiritual well-being.

Candles are simple yet profound tools that can transform a space and signify intention. The act of lighting a candle can be a ritual in itself, symbolizing the illumination of the mind and spirit. Different colors and scents of candles can align with specific intentions or deities. For instance, a white candle may represent purity and protection, while a green candle might be used for healing and prosperity. Using candles in meditation or prayer can help to focus the mind and create a serene atmosphere.

Mantras and affirmations are verbal tools that can shape your thoughts and energy. A mantra is a sacred word or phrase repeated during meditation, often in Sanskrit, that carries spiritual vibration. An affirmation is a positive statement that you repeat to yourself to instill a specific belief or intention. Examples of affirmations include "I am worthy of love and respect" or "I trust in the process of life." Regularly incorporating mantras or affirmations into your practice can reprogram your subconscious mind and align your energy with your desires.

Yoga mats and props are essential for those who incorporate physical movement into their spiritual practice. A quality yoga mat provides a comfortable and stable surface for asanas (postures) and can be used for meditation or relaxation as well. Props such as blocks, straps, and bolsters can support your practice by making poses more accessible and helping you maintain proper alignment. Incorporating a regular yoga practice can enhance your physical health, mental clarity, and spiritual connection.

The Power of Rituals

Rituals have long held a profound place in human existence, serving as a bridge between the mundane and the sacred. They offer a sense of structure, continuity, and meaning, providing a framework within which we can navigate the complexities of life. Whether rooted in religious tradition or personal spirituality, rituals can transform ordinary moments into sacred experiences, fostering a deeper connection to ourselves and the world around us.

Consider the simple act of lighting a candle. This seemingly mundane task can become a powerful ritual when performed with intention. As you strike the match and watch the flame flicker to life, you might take a moment to set an intention or offer a silent prayer. The light of the candle can symbolize illumination, hope, or the presence of the divine. By repeating this act regularly, it becomes imbued with personal significance, creating a moment of pause and reflection in the midst of your day.

Morning rituals can set the tone for the entire day, grounding you in a sense of purpose and calm before the busyness begins. Imagine waking up each morning and beginning with a few minutes of mindful breathing or gentle stretching. This small but intentional practice can help center your mind and body, preparing you to face the day with clarity and resilience. Incorporating elements such as journaling, where you jot down thoughts, dreams, or gratitude, can further enhance this ritual, providing a space to process emotions and set intentions.

Evening rituals, on the other hand, can serve as a way to unwind and reflect on the events of the day. Creating a nightly routine that includes activities like reading, meditating, or soaking in a warm bath can signal to your body and mind that it is time to relax and let go of the day's stresses. Reflecting on the day's experiences through a gratitude practice, where you list things you are thankful for, can shift your focus to the positive aspects of your life, fostering a sense of contentment and peace before sleep.

Seasonal rituals align us with the natural rhythms of the earth, marking the passage of time and the changing of seasons. Celebrating the solstices and equinoxes, for instance, can connect us to the cycles of nature and remind us of the ebb and flow of life. These rituals might include creating altars with seasonal elements, performing specific ceremonies, or spending time in nature to honor the transition. By acknowledging the changing seasons, we attune ourselves to the natural world and its inherent wisdom.

Life milestones are often marked by rituals that celebrate significant transitions and achievements. Weddings, births, and funerals are traditional examples, each accompanied by specific customs and ceremonies that provide a sense of continuity and community. Personal milestones, such as starting a new job, moving to a new home, or reaching a personal goal, can also be honored with rituals. Creating your own ceremonies to mark these occasions can add a deeper layer of meaning and acknowledgment to these significant moments in your life.

Daily routines can be transformed into rituals through mindfulness and intention. Consider the ritual of making tea or coffee in the morning. Instead of rushing through the process, you might take the time to savor each step: selecting your favorite mug, listening to the sound of the water boiling, and enjoying the aroma as you pour. This mindful approach turns a daily habit into a moment of presence and appreciation, grounding you in the present moment.

Rituals can also serve as a means of coping with change and uncertainty. During times of transition or difficulty, engaging in familiar and comforting rituals can provide a sense of stability and reassurance. Whether it's lighting a candle, reciting a prayer, or performing a simple act of kindness, these rituals can anchor us in the midst of chaos, offering a sense of continuity and hope.

Cultural rituals often carry deep historical and communal significance, connecting us to our heritage and the collective memory of our ancestors. Participating in cultural ceremonies and traditions can foster a sense of belonging and identity, linking us to a larger narrative that transcends our individual lives. These rituals might include celebrating holidays, observing traditional practices, or participating in community events that honor cultural heritage.

Creating your own rituals allows you to tailor them to your personal beliefs, values, and needs. These personalized rituals can be as simple or elaborate as you desire, reflecting what is meaningful to you. For example, you might create a ritual of walking in nature every Sunday morning, using this time to connect with the earth and reflect on the week ahead. Or you might develop a ritual of writing a letter to yourself on your birthday each year, reflecting on your growth and setting intentions for the coming year.

The power of rituals lies in their ability to create a sense of sacredness in our everyday lives. They offer a way to pause, reflect, and connect with something greater than ourselves, whether that be the divine, nature, or our own inner wisdom. By integrating rituals into our daily routines, we cultivate a deeper awareness and appreciation for the present moment, enriching our lives with meaning and purpose.

Incorporating rituals into your spiritual practice can be a deeply enriching and transformative experience. Start by identifying what resonates with you and what you hope to achieve through your rituals. Whether it's a sense of peace, clarity, connection, or gratitude, let this intention guide the creation and practice of your rituals. Remember that rituals are not about perfection or rigidity; they are about presence and intention. Allow them to evolve and adapt to your changing needs and circumstances, keeping them fresh and relevant to your journey.

To maintain the vitality of your rituals, revisit and renew them regularly. Reflect on how they are serving you and make adjustments as needed. You might find that certain rituals become more meaningful over time, while others may need to be replaced or refreshed. The key is to remain open and attentive to what feels right for you, allowing your rituals to grow and change alongside you.

Building a Support System

Navigating through life's challenges and triumphs can be significantly eased by having a strong support system. A support system, comprising friends, family, mentors, and community members, acts as a safety net, offering emotional, moral, and sometimes practical aid. Building such a network requires intentional effort, mutual respect, and ongoing maintenance, but the benefits are immeasurable.

Imagine embarking on a new career path or tackling a personal project. The journey can be daunting, filled with moments of doubt and uncertainty. With a support system in place, these moments become more manageable. Friends and family can provide encouragement and motivation, while mentors offer guidance and wisdom drawn from their own experiences. This collective support can bolster your confidence, making it easier to persevere through challenges.

Start by identifying the key people in your life who can form the foundation of your support system. These individuals should be those you trust and feel comfortable sharing your thoughts and feelings with. They might include family members who have always been there for you, friends who understand your aspirations, or colleagues who share your professional interests. This core group will form the bedrock upon which you can build a more extensive network.

Communication is the cornerstone of any strong support system. Regular and honest conversations help maintain these crucial relationships. Share your goals, fears, and successes with your support network, and be open to their feedback and advice. This two-way communication fosters trust and mutual respect, ensuring that everyone feels valued and heard.

Don't hesitate to reach out to new people who can add value to your support system. Join clubs, attend events, or participate in online communities related to your interests. These platforms provide opportunities to meet like-minded individuals who can offer fresh perspectives and support. For example, if you are passionate about writing, joining a local writers' group or an online forum can connect you with others who share your passion and can provide constructive feedback on your work.

Mentorship is a vital component of a robust support system. A mentor brings a wealth of experience and knowledge, offering guidance that can help you navigate complex situations and make informed decisions. Finding a mentor involves seeking out someone whose career or personal path you admire and respect. Approach them with a clear idea of what you hope to gain from the relationship, and be prepared to invest time and effort into nurturing this connection.

Reciprocity is key in any support system. It's not just about receiving help but also about offering support to others. Be there for your friends and family, offer your expertise to colleagues, and provide a listening ear to those who need it. This mutual exchange strengthens bonds and creates a sense of community and belonging.

Consider the role of professional support services in your network. Therapists, coaches, and counselors can provide specialized support that complements the help you receive from your personal connections. They offer a safe space to explore your thoughts and feelings, helping you develop strategies to cope with life's challenges. Investing in professional support can enhance your overall well-being and provide additional layers of support when needed.

Building a support system also involves setting boundaries. It's important to recognize when a relationship is no longer supportive or when someone's presence in your life is detrimental to your well-being. Setting clear boundaries helps protect your mental and emotional health, ensuring that your support network remains a positive force in your life.

Cultural and community groups can play a significant role in your support system. These groups often share common values, traditions, and experiences, providing a sense of belonging and understanding. Engaging with your cultural or community group can offer additional support, whether through shared activities, celebrations, or mutual aid.

Maintaining a support system requires ongoing effort and commitment. Regularly check in with your network, express gratitude for their support, and be mindful of their needs as well. This continuous nurturing of relationships ensures that your support system remains strong and resilient over time.

Technology can be a valuable tool in maintaining and expanding your support system. Social media, messaging apps, and video calls make it easier to stay connected with people, regardless of geographical distances. Use these tools to keep in touch with friends and family, join online communities, and participate in virtual events. However, be mindful of the quality of your interactions, aiming for meaningful connections rather than superficial ones.

Reflect on the impact your support system has on your life. Take note of how these relationships influence your mood, motivation, and overall well-being. This reflection can help you identify any gaps in your support network and guide you in seeking out additional connections or resources to fill those gaps.

In moments of crisis or significant change, your support system becomes even more crucial. Whether you're dealing with a personal loss, a health issue, or a major life transition, having a network of supportive individuals can provide the strength and resilience needed to get through tough times. Don't hesitate to lean on your support system during these moments, and remember that asking for help is a sign of strength, not weakness.

Building and maintaining a support system is a dynamic process that evolves over time. As your life circumstances change, so too will your support needs. Be open to adapting your network, welcoming new members, and letting go of relationships that no longer serve you. This flexibility ensures that your support system remains relevant and effective, providing the help and encouragement you need at every stage of your life.

Chapter 3

Awakening Your Inner Spirit

Recognizing the Call to Awaken

The journey of self-discovery often begins with a subtle yet profound moment of realization—a call to awaken. This call can manifest in many forms, from an inexplicable sense of longing to a sudden shift in perspective. Recognizing this call is the first step toward a deeper understanding of oneself and the world. It's a moment that invites you to pause, reflect, and embark on a path of spiritual and personal growth.

Imagine a typical day, filled with routine activities and familiar patterns. Then, out of nowhere, you experience a moment of clarity that disrupts the monotony. Perhaps it's a sense of dissatisfaction with your current situation, a feeling that there's more to life than what you've been experiencing. This moment, often described as an "awakening," is a powerful catalyst for change. It nudges you to explore new possibilities and question long-held beliefs.

For some, this call to awaken comes through a significant life event—a loss, a new opportunity, or a chance encounter. These events can shake you out of complacency, prompting you to reevaluate your life's direction. Take the story of Maria, for example. She had a stable job and a comfortable life but felt an underlying sense of emptiness. It wasn't until she lost a close friend that she began to question the purpose of her existence. This loss, though painful, became the impetus for her spiritual journey. She started meditating, reading spiritual texts, and seeking out like-minded individuals. Over time, Maria found a deeper sense of fulfillment and purpose.

Recognizing the call to awaken often involves tuning into your inner voice—the quiet yet persistent part of you that knows your true desires and potential. This inner voice can be drowned out by the noise of daily life, but it's always there, waiting to be heard. Learning to listen to this voice requires mindfulness and self-awareness. Practices like meditation, journaling, and spending time in nature can help you connect with your inner self and recognize the subtle cues that signal a call to awaken.

Sometimes, the call to awaken is not a single moment but a series of gentle nudges. These can be feelings of restlessness, curiosity, or a yearning for something more meaningful. Pay attention to these feelings, as they are often the first signs of an awakening. For instance, if you find yourself increasingly drawn to activities that nourish your soul—like art, music, or volunteering—it might be a sign that your spirit is awakening to a deeper purpose.

Embracing the call to awaken requires courage and a willingness to step out of your comfort zone. It's a journey that can challenge your existing beliefs and push you to confront fears and uncertainties. However, it is also a journey filled with profound rewards. As you begin to awaken, you'll start noticing synchronicities—meaningful coincidences that guide you along your path. These synchronicities can appear as chance meetings with people who inspire you, books that resonate with your current thoughts, or unexpected opportunities that align with your new direction.

Consider the story of John, who had always followed a conventional path. He went to college, secured a good job, and climbed the corporate ladder. Despite his success, John felt a persistent sense of dissatisfaction. One day, while on a business trip, he met an old acquaintance who had left a lucrative career to travel and pursue a simpler life. This encounter sparked something in John. He started questioning his own choices and realized he had been living according to societal expectations rather than his own desires. Inspired by the conversation, John gradually made changes in his life. He took up painting, a passion he had abandoned in his youth, and eventually transitioned to a career that aligned more closely with his true interests.

Recognizing the call to awaken often involves letting go of the fear of change. It's natural to feel apprehensive about stepping into the unknown, but embracing this uncertainty is essential for growth. Trusting the process and having faith in your journey can help you navigate the challenges that come with awakening. Remember that every step you take, no matter how small, brings you closer to a more authentic and fulfilling life.

Another key aspect of recognizing the call to awaken is being open to learning and growth. Awakening is not a one-time event but a continuous process of self-discovery and evolution. It involves constantly seeking new knowledge, experiences, and perspectives. This openness allows you to expand your consciousness and deepen your understanding of yourself and the world around you.

Community and support play a crucial role in the awakening process. Surrounding yourself with people who understand and support your journey can provide encouragement and guidance. Seek out communities, both online and offline, where you can share your experiences and learn from others. These connections can offer valuable insights and help you stay motivated on your path.

As you progress on your journey, you might encounter periods of doubt or setbacks. These are natural parts of the awakening process and should not be seen as failures. Instead, view them as opportunities for growth and learning. Each challenge you face can teach you something valuable about yourself and your journey. Embrace these moments with compassion and patience, knowing that they are integral to your development.

Reflect on your experiences regularly. Taking time to contemplate your journey allows you to recognize patterns, understand your progress, and set new intentions. Practices like journaling or engaging in dialogues with trusted friends can help you process your experiences and gain deeper insights into your awakening.

Overcoming Resistance

Overcoming resistance is a vital part of any journey toward personal growth and fulfillment. Resistance comes in many forms—self-doubt, procrastination, fear of failure, and even external obstacles. It's the force that holds you back from pursuing your dreams and realizing your potential. Understanding and conquering this resistance is essential for making meaningful progress in any aspect of life.

Picture yourself standing at the edge of a vast, open field. On the other side lies your goal, your dream. However, between you and that dream is a dense forest, representing the resistance you must navigate. This forest is intimidating and full of unknowns, but crossing it is necessary to reach your destination. The first step to overcoming resistance is recognizing its presence and understanding the reasons behind it.

Resistance often stems from fear—fear of the unknown, fear of failure, or even fear of success. These fears can paralyze you, making it difficult to take the first step toward your goals. Consider the story of Sarah, an aspiring writer who dreamed of publishing her first novel. Despite her passion and talent, Sarah found herself avoiding the blank page, overwhelmed by the fear of not being good enough. This fear, a common form of resistance, kept her from starting her manuscript for years.

To overcome such fears, it's important to confront them directly. Start by acknowledging your fears and understanding that they are a natural part of the human experience. Everyone faces resistance at some point, and recognizing this can help you feel less isolated in your struggles. Once you've identified your fears, challenge them. Ask yourself what's the worst that could happen if you fail. Often, the imagined consequences are far more daunting than reality. By breaking down these fears, you can diminish their power over you.

Another common form of resistance is self-doubt. This manifests as a persistent inner critic that questions your abilities and worth. Self-doubt can be crippling, preventing you from taking risks or pursuing opportunities. It's the voice that says, "You're not good enough," or "You don't have what it takes." Overcoming self-doubt requires cultivating a mindset of self-compassion and confidence. Start by focusing on your strengths and past achievements. Remind yourself of the times when you succeeded despite doubts. Surround yourself with supportive people who believe in you and your abilities. Their encouragement can help silence the inner critic and boost your confidence.

Procrastination is another form of resistance that can derail your progress. It's the act of delaying tasks, often until the last minute, which creates unnecessary stress and hampers your productivity. Procrastination is often rooted in perfectionism—the fear of not doing something perfectly can lead you to avoid doing it at all. To combat procrastination, adopt a mindset of progress over perfection. Accept that making mistakes is a part of the learning process and that it's better to make gradual progress than to remain stagnant. Break tasks into smaller, manageable steps, and set realistic deadlines for each. This approach makes daunting tasks feel more achievable and reduces the temptation to procrastinate.

External obstacles can also contribute to resistance. These may include lack of resources, unsupportive environments, or societal pressures. Overcoming external resistance involves finding creative solutions and seeking support. For instance, if you lack time due to a demanding job, look for ways to incorporate small steps toward your goal into your daily routine. If your environment is unsupportive, seek out communities or networks that share your interests and values. These external sources of support can provide motivation and practical assistance, helping you navigate obstacles more effectively.

A powerful tool for overcoming resistance is establishing a routine. Consistency can help build momentum and reduce the mental effort required to start tasks. For example, if you're working on a creative project, set aside a specific time each day dedicated solely to that project. Over time, this routine becomes a habit, making it easier to overcome initial resistance. Additionally, routines help create a sense of structure and discipline, which can be particularly useful when working toward long-term goals.

Visualization is another effective technique for overcoming resistance. By vividly imagining the successful completion of your goals, you can create a mental image that motivates and inspires you. Visualization helps bridge the gap between your current state and your desired outcome, making the goal feel more attainable. For instance, athletes often use visualization to picture themselves winning a race or achieving a personal best. This mental rehearsal prepares them for success and reduces resistance by fostering a positive mindset.

Accountability is crucial in overcoming resistance. Sharing your goals with someone else can provide an additional layer of motivation. This person can hold you accountable, check in on your progress, and offer encouragement when you encounter setbacks. Whether it's a friend, family member, or mentor, having someone who supports your journey can make a significant difference in overcoming resistance.

Self-care is an often-overlooked aspect of overcoming resistance. Taking care of your physical, emotional, and mental well-being can enhance your resilience and ability to tackle challenges. Regular exercise, healthy eating, adequate sleep, and mindfulness practices like meditation can boost your energy levels and reduce stress, making it easier to face resistance head-on.

Reflecting on your progress is essential for overcoming resistance. Regularly take time to review your achievements, reassess your goals, and adjust your strategies as needed. This reflection helps you stay aligned with your purpose and recognize the progress you've made, which can be incredibly motivating. It also allows you to identify any new forms of resistance that may arise and develop strategies to address them.

Lastly, persistence is key to overcoming resistance. The journey toward your goals is rarely a straight path; it's filled with ups and downs, detours, and setbacks. Persistence involves maintaining your commitment and continuing to move forward, even when faced with challenges. It's about developing a growth mindset—viewing obstacles as opportunities for learning and growth rather than insurmountable barriers. Embrace the process, celebrate small victories, and keep pushing toward your goals, knowing that each step brings you closer to overcoming resistance and achieving your dreams.

Daily Practices for Awakening

Waking up each day with a sense of purpose and clarity can transform your life. Daily practices for awakening are about cultivating habits that align your mind, body, and spirit to foster a deeper connection with your true self. These practices are not just routines but intentional actions that promote awareness, mindfulness, and growth. Integrating these into your daily life can help you navigate challenges more effectively and maintain a balanced, fulfilling existence.

Begin each day with a morning ritual that sets a positive tone. The way you start your morning can significantly impact your entire day. Consider incorporating practices such as meditation, journaling, or gentle stretching. Meditation helps quiet the mind, allowing you to begin the day with a sense of peace and centeredness. Even five to ten minutes of focused breathing can clear mental clutter and set a calm, intentional pace for the day.

Journaling in the morning can also be a powerful tool for self-reflection and goal setting. Writing down your thoughts, dreams, and intentions provides clarity and direction. It's a space where you can freely express yourself without judgment. This practice helps you process emotions and ideas, making it easier to approach the day with a clear and focused mind. Reflect on what you are grateful for, set positive intentions, and outline your goals for the day. This creates a mindset of abundance and purpose from the moment you wake up.

Incorporating movement into your morning routine can invigorate your body and mind. Whether it's a brisk walk, yoga, or simple stretching exercises, physical activity stimulates blood flow and releases endorphins, boosting your mood and energy levels. Movement also connects you to your body, fostering a sense of physical awareness that can enhance your overall well-being. Choose activities that you enjoy and that fit seamlessly into your schedule, ensuring that you start your day on a positive and energized note.

Mindful eating is another daily practice that can significantly impact your awakening journey. Paying attention to what you eat and how you eat can transform your relationship with food and your body. Begin by choosing whole, nutritious foods that nourish your body. Take time to savor each bite, eating slowly and mindfully. This practice not only enhances your physical health but also promotes a deeper connection with your body's signals and needs. By being present during meals, you develop a greater appreciation for the nourishment you receive and cultivate a sense of gratitude.

Throughout the day, practice mindfulness by bringing your full attention to the present moment. Whether you're working, interacting with others, or engaging in daily tasks, strive to be fully present. This means letting go of distractions and focusing on the task at hand. Mindfulness reduces stress, increases productivity, and enhances your overall sense of well-being. One effective way to practice mindfulness is through mindful breathing. Taking a few deep breaths at regular intervals throughout the day can help you stay grounded and centered, especially during stressful or busy moments.

Another powerful daily practice is setting aside time for reflection and self-inquiry. This can be done through journaling, meditation, or simply taking a quiet moment to ponder your thoughts and experiences. Reflecting on your day, your actions, and your emotions helps you gain insights into your patterns and behaviors. It allows you to identify areas of growth and areas that need adjustment. Self-inquiry encourages a deeper understanding of yourself and promotes continuous personal development.

Connecting with nature is an essential practice for awakening. Spending time outdoors, whether in a park, a garden, or by the sea, can have a profound impact on your mental and emotional well-being. Nature has a calming effect, helping to reduce stress and anxiety. It also fosters a sense of awe and interconnectedness, reminding you of the larger world beyond your daily concerns. Make it a habit to spend at least a few minutes each day outside, observing and appreciating the natural world around you.

Cultivating gratitude is another cornerstone of daily practices for awakening. Gratitude shifts your focus from what is lacking in your life to what is abundant. It fosters a positive mindset and enhances your overall sense of well-being. Each day, take a moment to reflect on the things you are grateful for, no matter how small. This practice can be integrated into your morning or evening routine, or even sprinkled throughout your day. By consistently acknowledging the positive aspects of your life, you create a habit of optimism and appreciation.

Building strong, meaningful connections with others is also crucial for your awakening journey. Engage in authentic, compassionate interactions with friends, family, and colleagues. Listen actively and speak from the heart. These connections provide support, encouragement, and perspective. They remind you that you are not alone on your journey and that you are part of a larger community. Make time for meaningful conversations and activities that strengthen your relationships and foster a sense of belonging.

Incorporating creative expression into your daily routine can also aid in your awakening. Whether it's through art, music, writing, or any other form of creativity, expressing yourself allows you to tap into your inner world and bring it into the external world. Creativity fosters self-discovery and can be a therapeutic way to process emotions and experiences. Set aside time each day to engage in a creative activity that brings you joy and fulfillment.

Evening rituals are just as important as morning routines in supporting your awakening. As the day winds down, create a calming routine that helps you transition into a restful state. This can include activities such as reading, taking a warm bath, or practicing gentle yoga or meditation. Reflect on your day, acknowledging your achievements and learning from your experiences. Setting aside time for relaxation and reflection in the evening prepares you for restful sleep and sets a positive tone for the next day.

Sleep is a fundamental aspect of daily practices for awakening. Quality sleep rejuvenates your body and mind, allowing you to function at your best. Establish a regular sleep schedule, aiming for seven to nine hours of sleep each night. Create a sleep-friendly environment by keeping your bedroom cool, dark, and quiet. Avoid screens and stimulating activities before bed, and instead, engage in calming practices that signal to your body that it's time to rest. Prioritizing sleep enhances your overall well-being and supports your ability to engage fully in your daily practices.

Lastly, practice self-compassion and patience. Awakening is a journey, not a destination. There will be days when you struggle to maintain your practices, and that's okay. Be gentle with yourself and recognize that growth takes time. Celebrate your progress, no matter how small, and keep moving forward with a sense of curiosity and openness. Self-compassion fosters resilience and encourages a positive, nurturing relationship with yourself.

The Role of Meditation

Meditation is more than just a practice; it is a journey into the depths of your own mind, a path to inner peace, clarity, and understanding. In a world that constantly demands our attention and energy, meditation offers a sanctuary, a place where you can retreat to reconnect with your true self. The benefits of meditation are vast, encompassing mental, emotional, and physical well-being. Understanding the role of meditation can help you incorporate it into your daily life, reaping its profound benefits.

One of the primary roles of meditation is to cultivate mindfulness. Mindfulness is the practice of being fully present in the moment, aware of your thoughts, feelings, and surroundings without judgment. This heightened awareness can transform your experience of life, allowing you to engage more deeply with the present. By regularly practicing meditation, you train your mind to return to this state of mindfulness, even amid the chaos of daily life. This can lead to improved focus, increased productivity, and a greater sense of calm.

Meditation also plays a crucial role in stress reduction. When you meditate, you activate the body's relaxation response, counteracting the stress response that often governs our lives. This not only reduces the immediate feelings of stress but also helps to lower blood pressure, improve heart health, and boost the immune system. Over time, regular meditation practice can significantly decrease overall stress levels, making you more resilient in the face of life's challenges.

Emotional regulation is another key benefit of meditation. By observing your thoughts and feelings without attachment or judgment, you gain a greater understanding of your emotional landscape. This can help you respond to situations with greater calm and clarity rather than reacting impulsively. Meditation teaches you to pause and reflect, creating a space between stimulus and response. This can be particularly beneficial in managing difficult emotions such as anger, anxiety, and sadness.

Meditation also enhances self-awareness. Through introspection, you begin to understand the patterns of your mind—your habitual thoughts, beliefs, and behaviors. This awareness can lead to personal growth and transformation. By recognizing these patterns, you can consciously choose to change them, fostering a more positive and constructive mindset. Self-awareness gained through meditation can also improve your relationships, as you become more attuned to your own needs and the needs of others.

Creativity and problem-solving skills can also be enhanced through meditation. When your mind is cluttered with constant thoughts and distractions, it can be challenging to think creatively or find solutions to problems. Meditation clears the mental clutter, allowing fresh ideas and insights to emerge. Many people find that their best ideas come to them during or after meditation. This state of relaxed awareness fosters a free flow of thoughts and ideas, unhampered by stress or overthinking.

In addition to mental and emotional benefits, meditation also impacts physical health. Regular meditation practice can improve sleep quality, reduce chronic pain, and even promote longevity. By reducing stress and promoting relaxation, meditation helps to balance the body's systems, leading to overall better health. It's a holistic practice that nurtures both the mind and the body, creating a state of harmony and balance.

There are various types of meditation, each with its own unique benefits and techniques. Mindfulness meditation, for example, focuses on being present and fully engaged in the current moment. This can be practiced by paying attention to your breath, bodily sensations, or even your thoughts and emotions as they arise. Loving-kindness meditation, on the other hand, involves cultivating feelings of compassion and love towards yourself and others. This practice can enhance empathy and improve your relationships.

Transcendental meditation involves the use of a mantra, a specific word or phrase, repeated silently to help focus the mind. This technique can lead to deep states of relaxation and heightened awareness. Guided meditation, where you listen to a guide who leads you through the practice, can be particularly helpful for beginners. Each type of meditation offers different pathways to achieving a state of inner peace and clarity.

Integrating meditation into your daily routine doesn't require a significant time commitment. Even just five to ten minutes a day can make a substantial difference. The key is consistency. Find a quiet space where you won't be disturbed, sit comfortably, and focus on your breath. If your mind wanders, gently bring it back to the breath without judgment. Over time, you will find it easier to stay focused and enter a meditative state.

To deepen your practice, consider joining a meditation group or attending a retreat. Meditating with others can provide additional support and motivation. Listening to others' experiences and sharing your own can be incredibly enriching. Retreats offer an immersive experience, allowing you to fully dedicate yourself to the practice, often leading to profound insights and breakthroughs.

Meditation can also be integrated into everyday activities. Walking meditation, for example, involves paying attention to the sensations of each step, the feeling of the ground beneath your feet, and the rhythm of your breath as you walk. This can turn a simple walk into a deeply mindful experience. Similarly, you can practice mindfulness while eating, paying full attention to the taste, texture, and aroma of your food, and the act of eating itself.

Meditation is a journey, and like any journey, it has its ups and downs. There will be days when your mind feels particularly restless, and meditation seems challenging. On other days, you may find it easier to slip into a state of deep calm and clarity. The important thing is to remain patient and compassionate with yourself. Every moment spent in meditation is valuable, contributing to your overall growth and well-being.

To maximize the benefits of meditation, it's helpful to keep a meditation journal. After each session, take a few minutes to jot down your experiences, any insights or thoughts that arose, and how you felt before and after the practice. This can help you track your progress and notice patterns over time. It also provides a space to reflect on your journey and celebrate your growth.

Visualization Techniques

Visualization techniques are powerful tools that harness the mind's ability to create vivid mental images, leading to enhanced performance, personal growth, and emotional well-being. By picturing a desired outcome or scenario, individuals can effectively program their subconscious mind to achieve specific goals. This chapter delves into the various methods and benefits of visualization, offering practical advice for beginners and seasoned practitioners alike.

One of the most effective ways to begin practicing visualization is through guided imagery. This technique involves listening to a narrator who describes a peaceful scene or a desired outcome, guiding you through the process of creating detailed mental images. For instance, you might be asked to imagine yourself walking through a serene forest, feeling the cool breeze on your skin, and hearing the rustling leaves. By engaging multiple senses, guided imagery helps to create a more immersive and convincing experience, making it easier for your mind to accept and work towards the visualized scenario.

Another popular technique is the creation of a vision board. A vision board is a collage of images, words, and symbols that represent your goals and aspirations. By placing this board in a location where you see it daily, you constantly remind yourself of your objectives, reinforcing your commitment to achieving them. The process of creating a vision board itself can be incredibly motivating, as it requires you to clarify your goals and identify the steps needed to reach them. Over time, the repeated exposure to these visual cues can significantly influence your thoughts, emotions, and actions, bringing you closer to your desired outcomes.

Mental rehearsal is a visualization technique commonly used by athletes, performers, and professionals to enhance their skills and prepare for high-pressure situations. This method involves vividly imagining yourself performing a task or activity, step by step, as if you were actually doing it. For example, a basketball player might mentally rehearse making free throws, visualizing the ball leaving their hands and swishing through the net. By repeatedly practicing in their mind, they can improve their muscle memory, boost their confidence, and reduce anxiety. Mental rehearsal can be applied to virtually any area of life, from giving a presentation to acing an exam, making it a versatile and valuable tool.

Creative visualization is another approach that emphasizes the importance of positive thinking and emotional engagement. In this technique, you not only visualize the desired outcome but also immerse yourself in the positive feelings associated with achieving it. For instance, if your goal is to land your dream job, you would imagine yourself receiving the job offer, feeling the excitement and pride, and experiencing the joy of telling your friends and family. By generating these positive emotions, you create a powerful connection between your mind and your goal, increasing your motivation and likelihood of success.

To maximize the effectiveness of visualization, it is crucial to practice regularly and with intention. Set aside dedicated time each day to engage in your chosen visualization technique, whether it's guided imagery, vision boarding, mental rehearsal, or creative visualization. Consistency is key, as the more you practice, the more ingrained the visualized scenarios become in your subconscious mind. Additionally, strive to make your visualizations as vivid and detailed as possible, incorporating all your senses and emotions to create a more realistic and compelling experience.

Visualization can also be enhanced by combining it with other complementary practices, such as meditation and affirmations. Meditation helps to quiet the mind, making it easier to focus on and sustain your visualizations. By practicing mindfulness, you can increase your awareness and control over your thoughts, reducing distractions and enhancing the clarity of your mental images. Affirmations, on the other hand, are positive statements that reinforce your goals and beliefs. By repeating affirmations in conjunction with your visualizations, you can strengthen the neural pathways associated with your desired outcomes, further embedding them in your subconscious mind.

One of the most fascinating aspects of visualization is its ability to influence the brain and body on a physiological level. Research has shown that the brain often cannot distinguish between a vividly imagined experience and a real one. When you visualize an activity, your brain activates the same neural pathways as it would if you were actually performing the task. This phenomenon, known as neuroplasticity, allows you to effectively "train" your brain through visualization, enhancing your skills and abilities over time.

In addition to improving performance, visualization can also be a powerful tool for healing and personal growth. For example, individuals dealing with chronic pain or illness can use visualization to imagine their body healing and recovering. By focusing on positive images of health and well-being, they can reduce stress, boost their immune system, and promote a sense of hope and empowerment. Similarly, visualization can help individuals overcome fears and phobias by gradually exposing them to the feared object or situation in a safe and controlled mental environment.

Visualization is not limited to individual practice; it can also be a valuable tool in group settings. Team visualization exercises can foster a sense of unity and shared purpose, enhancing collaboration and performance. For instance, a sports team might visualize winning a game together, imagining the strategies, movements, and emotions involved in achieving victory. By aligning their mental imagery and intentions, team members can strengthen their bond and work more effectively towards their common goal.

It's important to recognize that visualization is a skill that improves with practice. Beginners may find it challenging to create clear and vivid mental images at first, but with time and persistence, their ability to visualize will strengthen. If you find it difficult to visualize, try starting with simple and familiar images, gradually increasing the complexity as your skills improve. Additionally, don't be discouraged if your mind wanders during visualization sessions; simply acknowledge the distraction and gently bring your focus back to the mental images.

While visualization can be a powerful tool, it's essential to approach it with realistic expectations. Visualization alone is unlikely to produce miraculous results; it should be used in conjunction with concrete actions and efforts towards your goals. Think of visualization as a mental rehearsal that prepares and motivates you for the real-world steps you need to take. By combining the power of your mind with purposeful action, you can create a synergistic effect that propels you towards success.

Chapter 4

Discovering True Enlightenment

What is Enlightenment?

Enlightenment is often described as the ultimate goal of spiritual and personal development, a state of profound understanding, inner peace, and liberation. The concept of enlightenment varies across different cultures and traditions, but it commonly involves transcending ordinary human consciousness and achieving a higher level of awareness. This chapter delves into the essence of enlightenment, its significance, and practical steps to cultivate this elevated state of being.

The journey towards enlightenment often begins with a sense of dissatisfaction or a yearning for something beyond the material aspects of life. Individuals may feel that there is more to existence than the daily grind of work, relationships, and routine activities. This inner longing prompts a search for deeper meaning and truth. Enlightenment is not merely an intellectual understanding but a direct, experiential realization of the fundamental nature of reality.

Historically, enlightenment has been a central theme in many spiritual traditions. In Buddhism, it is known as Nirvana, a state of complete liberation from suffering and the cycle of rebirth. The Buddha, Siddhartha Gautama, attained enlightenment under the Bodhi tree after years of meditation and ascetic practices. His teachings emphasize the Four Noble Truths and the Eightfold Path as the means to achieve this state. Similarly, in Hinduism, enlightenment or Moksha signifies freedom from the cycle of birth and death (samsara) and union with the divine. The Bhagavad Gita, a sacred Hindu text, outlines various paths to enlightenment, including devotion (bhakti), knowledge (jnana), and disciplined action (karma).

In the context of Western philosophy, enlightenment took on a different connotation during the 18th century European Enlightenment period. It was characterized by an emphasis on reason, science, and intellectual exploration. Thinkers like Immanuel Kant, who famously defined enlightenment as "man's emergence from his self-imposed immaturity," advocated for the use of reason as the path to personal and societal progress. However, this intellectual enlightenment differs from the spiritual enlightenment sought in Eastern traditions, which focuses on transcending the ego and experiencing unity with the cosmos.

Regardless of cultural or philosophical context, a common thread in descriptions of enlightenment is the dissolution of the ego, the sense of a separate self. This shift in perception reveals the interconnectedness of all life and the underlying unity of existence. The ego, with its constant desires, fears, and attachments, is seen as the primary obstacle to enlightenment. By transcending the ego, one can experience a state of pure awareness, free from the distortions of personal biases and limitations.

Meditation is one of the most widely recognized practices for cultivating enlightenment. Through meditation, individuals can quiet the mind, observe their thoughts without attachment, and gradually dismantle the ego's hold. Techniques such as mindfulness meditation, where one focuses on the present moment without judgment, and transcendental meditation, which involves the repetition of a mantra, are popular methods. Regular meditation practice can lead to profound insights, inner peace, and a heightened sense of presence.

Another essential aspect of the path to enlightenment is self-inquiry or introspection. This involves questioning the nature of the self and reality. In Advaita Vedanta, a non-dualistic school of Hindu philosophy, the practice of self-inquiry (Atma Vichara) is central. It involves the continuous contemplation of the question, "Who am I?" By peeling away the layers of identification with the body, mind, and personality, one can discover the true self, which is beyond all physical and mental constructs.

Living ethically and cultivating virtues such as compassion, humility, and gratitude are also crucial components of the journey towards enlightenment. Ethical conduct purifies the mind and creates a harmonious environment conducive to spiritual growth. Compassion, in particular, is emphasized in many traditions. By extending kindness and understanding to others, one can transcend the ego's narrow focus on self-interest and experience a sense of unity with all beings.

The role of a teacher or guide can be invaluable in the pursuit of enlightenment. Throughout history, enlightened masters and gurus have provided guidance, support, and inspiration to seekers. Their teachings, presence, and personal example can help illuminate the path and dispel doubts. However, it is essential for each individual to take personal responsibility for their journey and not become overly dependent on any external source.

While the path to enlightenment is deeply personal, it often involves stages or milestones. Initially, seekers may experience fleeting glimpses of expanded awareness or moments of profound peace.

These experiences can provide motivation and confirmation of the path. Over time, with sustained practice and commitment, these glimpses can become more frequent and stable, eventually leading to a permanent shift in consciousness.

It is important to acknowledge that the path to enlightenment is not always smooth or linear. Seeker's may encounter challenges, doubts, and periods of stagnation. These obstacles can be valuable opportunities for growth and learning. Patience, perseverance, and a sense of humor can help navigate the ups and downs of the journey.

One of the profound realizations that often accompanies enlightenment is the understanding of impermanence. Everything in the physical and mental realm is transient, constantly changing and evolving. By accepting this impermanence, one can let go of attachment and aversion, which are sources of suffering. This acceptance leads to a state of equanimity, where one can remain peaceful and balanced amidst the fluctuations of life.

Another key aspect of enlightenment is the experience of unconditional love. This love is not limited to romantic or familial relationships but extends to all beings and the entire universe. It is a recognition of the inherent divinity and worth of every aspect of creation. This boundless love fosters a deep sense of connection and compassion, transforming how one interacts with the world.

Ultimately, enlightenment is not an endpoint but an ongoing process of unfolding and deepening awareness. It is a journey of self-discovery and transformation that can continue throughout one's life. Each moment, each experience, offers an opportunity to awaken further and embody the qualities of wisdom, compassion, and love.

Incorporating the principles and practices conducive to enlightenment into daily life can lead to profound changes. By dedicating time to meditation, engaging in self-inquiry, living ethically, and cultivating virtues, one can create a fertile ground for spiritual growth. Embracing the journey with an open heart and a curious mind allows for the continuous exploration of the vast and mysterious landscape of consciousness.

Stages of Enlightenment

Embarking on the journey to enlightenment is akin to setting off on an epic voyage across uncharted waters. This path, marked by various stages and milestones, guides seekers through a transformative process that gradually unfolds their highest potential. Understanding these stages can provide clarity, direction, and motivation for those committed to exploring the depths of their consciousness.

The initial stage of enlightenment often begins with a sense of dissatisfaction or a deep inner yearning. This dissatisfaction isn't necessarily tied to external circumstances but rather stems from a feeling that there is more to life than what meets the eye. This stage, known as the "Call to Adventure," is characterized by a growing awareness that the material world and its pursuits cannot fully satisfy the soul's deeper longings.

This awakening prompts individuals to seek answers, leading them to explore various spiritual practices, philosophies, and teachings. It's a period of significant curiosity and openness, where one might experiment with meditation, read sacred texts, or attend spiritual workshops. This stage is crucial as it lays the foundation for the entire journey, opening the door to a broader perspective of life and existence.

As seekers delve deeper into their spiritual practices, they enter the stage of "Purification and Self-Discipline." Here, the focus shifts towards cleansing the mind and body of impurities that hinder spiritual growth. This stage often involves adopting a disciplined lifestyle, including regular meditation, ethical living, and mindful consumption of food and media. By purifying the mind and body, individuals create a conducive environment for deeper spiritual experiences.

During this stage, one might encounter the "Dark Night of the Soul," a period of intense inner turmoil and confusion. This is a time when deeply ingrained fears, doubts, and unresolved traumas surface, challenging the seeker to confront and release them. Although this phase can be incredibly challenging, it is also transformative. It serves as a powerful catalyst for growth, helping individuals shed the layers of ego and false identities that obscure their true nature.

Emerging from the Dark Night of the Soul, seekers enter the stage of "Illumination." This is characterized by moments of profound insight and clarity, where the interconnectedness of all life becomes apparent. These glimpses of higher consciousness can be fleeting at first but grow more frequent and stable with continued practice. During this stage, individuals often experience heightened intuition, synchronicities, and a deep sense of peace and contentment.

Illumination is not the final destination but rather a significant milestone on the path to enlightenment. It is a period of great joy and inspiration, where the truths of existence are no longer abstract concepts but direct experiences. Seekers feel a deep connection to all beings and a sense of purpose that transcends personal desires and ambitions.

Following Illumination, the journey continues with the stage of "Surrender and Non-Attachment." Here, the focus shifts towards letting go of all remaining attachments and desires that bind one to the egoic mind. This stage requires a profound level of trust and surrender to the flow of life. By relinquishing control and embracing uncertainty, individuals can experience a state of inner freedom and liberation.

During this stage, the practice of non-attachment becomes central. It involves letting go of the need to cling to people, possessions, and outcomes, recognizing that everything in the material world is transient. This doesn't mean becoming indifferent or apathetic but rather engaging with life from a place of inner fullness and contentment. Non-attachment allows individuals to experience life more fully, without the constant fear of loss or disappointment.

As seekers deepen their practice of surrender and non-attachment, they move into the stage of "Unity Consciousness." This is a state of profound oneness with all of creation, where the boundaries between self and other dissolve. In Unity Consciousness, individuals experience themselves as part of the universal fabric of existence, interconnected with all beings and the cosmos. This stage is characterized by unconditional love, compassion, and a sense of boundless joy.

Unity Consciousness is often accompanied by a sense of timelessness and presence. The past and future lose their grip, and the present moment becomes the primary focus. This state of being allows individuals to engage with life more fully, appreciating the beauty and wonder of each moment. It also fosters a deep sense of empathy and compassion, as the suffering and joy of others are felt as one's own.

The final stage of enlightenment is "Embodiment and Integration." Here, the insights and experiences gained throughout the journey are integrated into everyday life. Enlightenment is not about escaping the world but about living fully and authentically within it. This stage involves embodying the qualities of wisdom, compassion, and love in all aspects of life, from personal relationships to professional endeavors.

Embodiment and Integration require a balance between the inner and outer worlds. It involves maintaining a deep connection to one's inner self while engaging with the external world with clarity and purpose. This stage is about bringing the light of enlightenment into the mundane, transforming ordinary activities into expressions of divine presence.

One of the key aspects of this stage is service to others. Enlightened individuals often feel a profound calling to contribute to the well-being of all beings. This service can take many forms, from teaching and mentoring to social activism and creative expression. By sharing their insights and gifts, enlightened individuals help uplift and inspire others on their journey.

The stages of enlightenment are not linear but cyclical. Seekers may revisit different stages at various points in their journey, each time gaining deeper insights and understanding. The path to enlightenment is unique for each individual, shaped by their experiences, temperament, and destiny.

It is essential to approach the journey with patience, perseverance, and a sense of humility. Enlightenment is not a destination to be reached but a continuous unfolding of one's true nature. By staying committed to the path and embracing each stage with openness and curiosity, individuals can experience the profound transformation that enlightenment offers.

Myths and Misconceptions

The journey towards understanding and achieving personal growth is often clouded by myths and misconceptions. These misconceptions can hinder progress, create unnecessary obstacles, and discourage genuine seekers from continuing their quest. To navigate this path effectively, it is crucial to debunk these myths and replace them with a more accurate understanding.

One of the most pervasive myths is the idea that personal growth is a linear process. Many believe that progress is a straight path, moving steadily from one point to another. However, personal growth is more akin to a spiral, often involving revisiting issues, learning new lessons, and sometimes feeling as though one is moving backward. This non-linear nature is natural and should be embraced rather than resisted. Each step, whether forward or seemingly backward, contributes to the overall journey and deepens understanding.

Another common misconception is that personal growth requires drastic changes in one's life circumstances. While dramatic transformations can be a part of the process, personal growth often involves subtle shifts in perception, attitude, and behavior. It's about cultivating awareness and making mindful choices in everyday situations. Small, consistent changes can have a profound impact over time, leading to significant growth without the need for radical upheaval.

There is also a myth that personal growth is a solitary journey. While personal reflection and individual effort are essential, the role of community and relationships cannot be overlooked. Engaging with others, sharing experiences, and learning from different perspectives enriches the journey. Supportive relationships provide encouragement, accountability, and insight, helping to navigate challenges and celebrate successes.

A particularly damaging misconception is that personal growth is solely about achieving happiness or a constant state of positivity. This belief can lead to the suppression of negative emotions and unrealistic expectations. True personal growth involves embracing the full spectrum of human experience, including pain, sorrow, and anger. These emotions are valuable teachers and integral to the process. By facing and integrating all aspects of oneself, deeper healing and transformation occur.

Many people also believe that personal growth is only for a select few, those with certain privileges or resources. This myth excludes many from even attempting to grow, believing it is beyond their reach. However, personal growth is accessible to everyone, regardless of background or circumstances. It is about making the best of where one is and using available resources to foster development. Books, online resources, community groups, and personal reflection are tools that anyone can utilize.

The idea that personal growth leads to perfection is another widespread myth. The pursuit of perfection can be paralyzing and counterproductive. Growth is about progress, not perfection. It involves accepting imperfections, learning from mistakes, and continuously striving to become a better version of oneself. Embracing imperfection allows for greater compassion towards oneself and others, fostering a more authentic and fulfilling journey.

Misconceptions about the time required for personal growth are also common. Some believe it's a quick fix, while others think it takes a lifetime. The truth lies somewhere in between. Personal growth is an ongoing process without a definitive endpoint. It requires patience, persistence, and a willingness to engage in lifelong learning. Setting realistic expectations about the time and effort involved can prevent frustration and disillusionment.

Another myth is that personal growth means always being in control. This belief can lead to rigidity and resistance to change. True growth often involves surrendering control, allowing life to unfold naturally, and adapting to new circumstances. Flexibility and openness to change are vital components of personal growth. By letting go of the need to control every outcome, individuals can experience greater freedom and resilience.

People often misconstrue personal growth as a purely intellectual exercise, involving only the mind and ignoring the body and emotions. This misconception overlooks the interconnectedness of mind, body, and spirit. Personal growth involves holistic development, addressing physical health, emotional well-being, and spiritual awareness. Practices such as mindfulness, exercise, and emotional processing are all essential aspects of a balanced growth journey.

There is also a myth that personal growth leads to a life free of challenges and difficulties. This misconception can create unrealistic expectations and disappointment. Challenges are an inherent part of life and personal growth. They provide opportunities for learning, resilience, and deeper understanding. Embracing challenges and viewing them as growth opportunities can shift the perspective from victimhood to empowerment.

The belief that personal growth is a one-size-fits-all process is another common misconception. Each individual's journey is unique, shaped by personal experiences, values, and goals. What works for one person may not work for another. It's important to honor one's unique path and explore various approaches to find what resonates most. Personal growth is a deeply personal journey that requires self-awareness and authenticity.

Finally, the myth that personal growth is a destination rather than a journey can limit one's experience. Viewing growth as a final goal to be achieved misses the essence of the process. Personal growth is a continuous, evolving journey of self-discovery and transformation. It's about embracing the present moment, learning from each experience, and continually striving towards greater understanding and fulfillment.

Personal Stories of Enlightenment

Sitting by the river under the canopy of ancient trees, Maya felt an inexplicable pull towards the flowing water. She had always been a seeker, yearning for a deeper understanding of life beyond the mundane routines. Her journey towards enlightenment began in her early twenties when she stumbled upon a book on Eastern philosophy. The concepts of mindfulness and presence resonated with her, sparking a curiosity that would shape her path for years to come.

Maya's first significant experience occurred during a retreat in the mountains. Surrounded by nature and away from the distractions of modern life, she immersed herself in meditation and self-reflection. One evening, as the sun set and the sky turned a deep shade of purple, she experienced a moment of profound clarity. It was as if a veil had been lifted, revealing the interconnectedness of all things. This fleeting but powerful insight set her on a transformative journey, teaching her that enlightenment is not a distant goal but a series of moments where the truth becomes unmistakably clear.

Similarly, Raj's path to enlightenment was marked by a series of personal trials. Growing up in a bustling city, he was constantly surrounded by noise and chaos. His life was filled with ambition and material pursuits, but a lingering sense of emptiness never left him. It was not until he faced a severe health crisis that he began to question his way of life. During his recovery, Raj turned to meditation and spiritual texts for solace. One particular meditation session changed everything. As he sat in silence, a profound sense of peace washed over him. He realized that his true essence was beyond his physical body and material possessions. This awakening prompted him to simplify his life, focusing on what truly mattered: inner peace and spiritual growth.

For Anya, enlightenment came through the practice of selfless service. Working in a high-stress corporate job, she often felt disconnected and unfulfilled. A chance encounter with a volunteer organization led her to spend weekends helping underprivileged children. The joy and gratitude she witnessed in their eyes sparked something within her. Anya began to understand that enlightenment is not only about personal awakening but also about contributing to the well-being of others. Her acts of kindness and service became a spiritual practice, teaching her that true fulfillment comes from giving selflessly and connecting with others on a deeper level.

Jamal's story is one of resilience and transformation. Born into a tumultuous environment, he faced numerous challenges from a young age. Despite the odds, he pursued education and found solace in music and poetry. His creative pursuits became a means of exploring his inner world and expressing his deepest emotions. One evening, while performing at a local café, he experienced a moment of oneness with his audience. The boundaries between him and the listeners seemed to dissolve, and he felt a profound connection with everyone present. This experience was a turning point, showing him that enlightenment could be found in moments of genuine expression and connection.

Elena's journey began with a deep sense of restlessness. Despite having a successful career and a loving family, she felt something was missing. She decided to take a sabbatical and travel to a remote monastery in Tibet. Immersed in the monastic lifestyle, she spent her days in meditation, contemplation, and study. One morning, as she walked through the serene monastery gardens, she was struck by the simple beauty of a blooming flower. In that moment, she experienced an overwhelming sense of presence and unity with all of existence. This realization changed her perspective, teaching her that enlightenment is not about escaping reality but embracing it fully, with an open heart and mind.

Carlos's enlightenment story is intertwined with nature. Growing up near the ocean, he always felt a deep connection to the sea. After a particularly stressful period in his life, he took a solo trip to a secluded beach. Spending his days swimming, meditating, and simply being present with the waves, he began to feel a profound sense of peace and clarity. One evening, as he watched the sunset paint the sky with vibrant colors, he had an epiphany. He realized that the ebb and flow of the tides mirrored the rhythms of life. This understanding helped him navigate life's challenges with greater ease, seeing them as natural cycles rather than obstacles.

Lila's path to enlightenment was marked by a deep dive into ancient wisdom. As a scholar of religious studies, she had always been fascinated by the teachings of mystics and sages. However, it wasn't until she began to practice what she studied that she experienced true transformation. Through daily meditation, prayer, and mindfulness practices, she cultivated a deep sense of inner stillness. One night, during a particularly intense meditation session, she felt a profound sense of unity with the universe. This experience dissolved her sense of separateness, revealing the interconnectedness of all beings. Lila's journey taught her that enlightenment is not about intellectual understanding but direct, lived experience.

Each of these stories illustrates that enlightenment is a deeply personal and unique journey. It is not confined to a specific path or practice but can be found in various aspects of life. Whether through moments of clarity, acts of service, creative expression, connection with nature, or immersion in ancient wisdom, enlightenment reveals itself in different ways to different people. The common thread is the profound sense of connection, presence, and inner peace that these experiences bring.

Achieving Higher Consciousness

The concept of higher consciousness often evokes images of mystics meditating on mountaintops or sages delivering profound wisdom. While these images hold a certain allure, achieving higher consciousness is not an exclusive pursuit reserved for the spiritually elite. It is an accessible journey that anyone can embark upon, regardless of background or lifestyle. This chapter delves into practical and actionable steps to elevate one's consciousness, transforming everyday life into a path of profound awareness and understanding.

Higher consciousness begins with the cultivation of mindfulness. Mindfulness, the practice of being fully present in each moment, serves as the foundation for expanding awareness. It involves observing thoughts, emotions, and sensations without judgment. Beginners can start by setting aside a few minutes each day to sit quietly and focus on their breath. This simple practice helps anchor the mind, reducing the constant chatter that obscures deeper insights. Over time, mindfulness can be integrated into daily activities, from eating to walking, turning mundane moments into opportunities for heightened awareness.

Meditation is another powerful tool for achieving higher consciousness. There are various forms of meditation, including focused attention, loving-kindness, and transcendental meditation. Each offers unique benefits, but all share the goal of quieting the mind and connecting with a deeper state of being. For beginners, guided meditations can be particularly helpful, providing structure and support. As one becomes more experienced, it may be beneficial to explore different techniques to find what resonates most deeply. Regular meditation practice not only enhances mental clarity but also fosters a profound sense of inner peace.

Engaging with nature is a simple yet profound way to elevate consciousness. Nature has a unique ability to ground us, reminding us of our interconnectedness with all life. Spending time outdoors, whether walking in a park, hiking in the mountains, or simply sitting by a river, can help clear the mind and open the heart. Nature's rhythms and cycles reflect the larger patterns of existence, offering insights that are often missed in the hustle and bustle of daily life. By attuning to the natural world, one can cultivate a deeper sense of harmony and presence.

Reading and studying spiritual texts can also be a gateway to higher consciousness. Many traditions offer profound teachings that have been passed down through the ages. Whether it's the Bhagavad Gita, the Tao Te Ching, or modern spiritual classics, these texts can provide valuable guidance and inspiration. It's important to approach these readings with an open mind and heart, allowing the wisdom to resonate and unfold naturally. Reflecting on and discussing these teachings with others can further deepen understanding and insight.

Self-inquiry is a powerful practice for those seeking higher consciousness. This involves asking profound questions about the nature of the self and existence.

Questions like "Who am I?" and "What is my true nature?" can lead to deep realizations when explored earnestly. Self-inquiry requires a willingness to look beyond surface identities and roles, delving into the essence of one's being. Journaling can be a helpful tool in this process, providing a space to explore thoughts and insights as they arise. Over time, self-inquiry can dissolve limiting beliefs and reveal a more expansive sense of self.

Cultivating compassion is essential on the path to higher consciousness. Compassion for oneself and others opens the heart and dissolves barriers that separate us. Acts of kindness, empathy, and understanding foster a sense of interconnectedness and unity. Practicing loving-kindness meditation, where one sends goodwill and loving thoughts to oneself and others, can help develop this quality. By seeing the divine in all beings, compassion becomes a natural expression of higher consciousness.

Another key aspect of achieving higher consciousness is letting go of attachment and aversion. These twin forces often dominate our lives, causing suffering and limiting our awareness. Attachment to material possessions, relationships, or outcomes creates a sense of dependence and anxiety. Aversion, on the other hand, involves pushing away experiences or emotions we find unpleasant. Both are rooted in the illusion of separation and the ego's need for control. By practicing non-attachment and acceptance, one can transcend these limitations and experience a greater sense of freedom and equanimity.

Maintaining a balanced lifestyle supports the journey towards higher consciousness. This includes regular physical exercise, a healthy diet, sufficient rest, and nurturing relationships. Physical well-being is closely linked to mental and spiritual health, and neglecting the body can hinder progress. Practices like yoga and tai chi, which integrate physical movement with mindfulness and breath awareness, can be particularly beneficial. Additionally, surrounding oneself with supportive and like-minded individuals can provide encouragement and inspiration on the path.

Higher consciousness also involves a deep appreciation for the present moment. The past and future often dominate our thoughts, pulling us away from the only moment that truly exists—the now. Practicing presence involves fully engaging with what is happening in the moment, whether it's a conversation, a task, or simply being. This doesn't mean ignoring responsibilities or planning for the future, but rather doing so with a grounded awareness. Techniques like mindful breathing and body scans can help anchor attention in the present, fostering a deeper sense of peace and clarity.

Engaging in creative activities can also elevate consciousness. Whether it's painting, writing, dancing, or playing music, creative expression allows for the flow of intuitive insights and deeper truths. It bypasses the analytical mind, tapping into a more expansive and connected state of awareness. For many, engaging in creative pursuits becomes a form of meditation, offering moments of transcendence and inspiration. It's important to approach these activities with a sense of playfulness and openness, allowing the creative process to unfold naturally.

Lastly, cultivating a sense of gratitude can significantly enhance consciousness. Gratitude shifts focus from what is lacking to what is abundant, opening the heart to the richness of life. Keeping a gratitude journal, where one regularly records things they are thankful for, can foster this mindset. By appreciating the beauty and blessings in each moment, one aligns with a higher frequency of awareness.

www.ingramcontent.com/pod-product-compliance
Lightning Source LLC
Chambersburg PA
CBHW061323120726
48001CB00002B/660